D1601511

FACING the MUSIC

Poems by Bruce Berger

[signature: Bruce Berger]

Confluence Press
Lewiston, Idaho

Library of Congress Catalogue Number: 94-069719

ISBN (paper) 1-881090-14-0

First Printing: May, 1995

Published by Confluence Press, 500 8th Avenue, Lewis-Clark State
College, Lewiston, Idaho 83501. James Anderson, Guest Editor.

Jacket art by Reginald Kell, from the author's collection. Jacket design by
Marilyn Auer.

Manufactured in the United States of America.

Acknowledgements

Certain of the poems in this collection have previously appeared in various magazines, as follows:

Barron's: "Money: A Primer"
Bird Watcher's Digest: "Birder"
Denver Quarterly: "Late Sibelius," "Myoptics"
Nebo: "Window Seats"
Negative Capability: "Gaspard," "Death Florentine," "Vespers"
New Letters: "Opus Posthumous," "Of Joe"

Poetry: "Facing the Music," "To Answer Your Question," "Impressionists," "Family Reading," "Opus 28, The Preludes," "Across, Down," "Don't Ask," "Enigma Variations," "These Arias," "The Wedding Gift"

Poetry Northwest: "Departure"
Skating: "Backward and Human"
Stone Country: "Social Rubato"

Aspen Music Festival: "Practice Rooms"

FOR
KURT OPPENS

Contents

Backward and Human

Coiling back to one foot,
Arms and free leg stretched out
And gradually drawing in,
The skater begins his spin
Feeling a gathered weight
Tighten, accelerate
As he loses shape and blends
Geometry squeezed toward its ends,
Adjusting, inventing form
With a head thrown back, an arm
Curled up, a resilient pole
Sculpting its mood, until
Momentum begins to lapse,
And before his spiral slips
And splinters the mirage
He steps to an outer edge,
Coming out of his spin
Backward and human again.

To Answer Your Question

Mozart or Beethoven, he asked by his five foot wall
Of records, German, an artist. Fresh from high school,
How should I know if I was supposed to prefer
Beethoven's central command and squared-off thunder
Or Mozart's sinuous charm? But the question had
A wrong answer, and was honed to see if I made
A suitable companion for his son.
The one *you* prefer, I said in desperation.
No, please, choose, he persisted with that faint
Hovering demismile that seemd to hint
Some terrifying dictum such as, "the boy
Reads Dostoevski while the man reads Tolstoi."
Whichever you like, truly, I stammered, maddeningly
Aware I'd found the wrong answer anyway,
But one that got us dismissed to music I can't
Recall, blissful breakfasters, ignorant
Of the deep inconsequence that flames into art.
To answer your question, Mr. Stephan, Mozart.

Gaspard

After glasses of Napa red had reduced us to quavers
Franc brought out his battered score of *Gaspard de la nuit.*
No matter you'll never play it, he said. It's yours.
Read through the easy parts, if you can find any,
But follow it close with the record until you can tell
How chords, progressions, runs, scraps of melody,
Structure itself are shivered, fractured, disjoined
Like moonlight tangled in crystal, starlight in sound.
After several more glasses I left, leaving *Gaspard,*
And went back shamefaced next morning to fetch it. The score
Lay shivered like fly-stained confetti across the floor.
I'd shown him utter contempt, not to mention Ravel.
Years later in Mexico, I learned from a friend,
Franc did what he'd long dreamt of, to secret laughter:
He put on his buckskin jacket and shot himself.
My notes for *Gaspard* are still only liner notes
On its three-movement program, clues for novice ears
To playing so wicked its quarry can almost see
Lighthearted Ondine luring her lovers to drown,
The gibbet that trembles every window in town
And tough little Scarbo, who dances and disappears.

3

Opus Posthumous

No summons was meant
But I cut the hair she didn't approve,
Phoned to say I was coming, and drove
Eight hundred miles southwest
To her terminal non-event:
Cremation without ceremony, by request.

No rite to set her descendants free?
I maneuvered a public meal, just
My mother, her fiancé, and me,
And in the lounge imposed a toast,
Stressing her gentler side, to the one
Grandparent I'd overlapped with, now gone.

Eight hundred miles back home, and there in the box
A letter in her spidery hand!
Word from beyond? "That man just takes
And will take your mother for all she's worth,
You must stop the marriage!" Was there no end
To her cursive suspicions, even in death?

No, postmarked the day *before* she died:
This ink simply slipped
Out last, but so breathlessly close it implied
Little change of heart, here or there.
I tore up her farewell script
And grew back my hair.

Family Reading

He tore the book from my mother's hand and glared:
"*Fashion Is Spinach*. You should be reading the classics!"
"But I did read the classics, in high school," she shot back,
Naming a level my father never reached.
"I even acted in a classic play,
Men For All, adapted from something else."
Precisely because he'd never cleared eighth grade
He spent a remedial lifetime laying claim
To Shakespeare, Dickens and Kipling, the three Britishers
Gifted with the juju to ripen a raw
Chicagoan. By the time his final child
Reached high school, less oxygen reached his brain;
Nonetheless I brought him an assigned book,
Moby Dick. He was off on his final voyage,
Breasting vapors of prose as his veins permitted,
Charting his spot with a scrap of *Chicago Tribune*
That yellowed as it advanced. Clearing his throat
To keep us anchored to his misting voice
He let the rhetoric rain, again and again,
On the coin nailed to the mast, as if obscurely
In the rust-spiked gold doubloon he saw reflected
The stilled reckoning of the CPA.
The last year emphysema let words through
At all, the splinter of newsprint only moved
From page 250 to 254,
Then the white whale dove forever beyond his ken.
"*Fashion Is Spinach* wasn't nearly as worthless
As your father liked to think," insists my mother.
"I still remember what I learned from it."

The Equation

All things can be reduced to mathematics,
She says, having one son in jail,
A husband strapped by his seatbelt to the flames,
Two overweight daughters and a second son
Genius turned junkie, for which she obscurely blames
Her own example, despising the money she makes
Tweaking the chips of war; and as she sits
Surrounded by hostile eyes at coffee breaks
She dreams of a world where all the trees have names,
Where words connote what they denote, where it's
Always mid-July and food doesn't run
To fat, where hair stays combed and conscience clean,
The animal lies down with the machine
And the noumena and phenomena are one.

Impressionists

These paintings Paris laughed down
A hundred years ago
Have finally found their salon.

In a house of sheer window
Stitched to a cliff's edge
In crystalline vertigo,

Street scenes from the age
Of the Grand Passion for Light
Hang to great advantage.

In silver frames over white
Wicker, off-white leather
And books of Monet and Cassatt,

Old plazas of rainy weather—
Soft underlit faces
Of shoppers sheltered together

And spaced by the rhythmic oases
Of black umbrellas—provide
Just the right resting places

For folks back from the wide
World that deepens a tan,
Companionably inside

In the quietly dancing sheen
Of sunlight swept to the eaves
By spangled Lake Michigan,

A dappled family runny
With leaves and blinding waves
Of water, light and money.

Facing the Music

Season by season the listener sits
In the fifteenth row and just to the left
Where frowns, bowings, fingerings, the conductor's
Downbeats, nods and attenuated slurs
Slip easily into the eye, where above all
The acoustics of the refurbished downtown hall
Bring heartbeat, hearing and a bi-monthly program
Into one consonance.

When did the prodigy mature, when
Did the virtuoso lose his edge?
Nights in focus blurred from year to year.
Sadly easier to pin down
The concertmaster's new beard, a cellist's chair
Rigged for a back problem, a huge bassoonist
Replaced by kid with moustache, the harpist's hair
Gone natural. Dizzyingly, the strings
Getting younger and younger. The influx
Of women, of Orientals. The first blacks.
An orchestra becoming the crowd in the street.

Change certified within the civic shell!
One guest conductor all theater and sweat,
Next month a mannikin. Far worse
The flawed appointment, perfectionist martinet
Endured a half-decade. Truly grave:
The year of the strike, the season nearly canceled.
Musicians as flight attendants? Or firemen?
Music as service, or product? The listener gave
And gave again.

Time shaped itself so differently each time:
The baroque chug, the impressionist swoon,
The yearly cold dip
Into twelve tone, the classical shrine's overblown
Facade. And somewhere in every line-up

A deeply involving theme
Withstood its trial by ravishment to return
In such pure celebration it was time
Itself, two nights in thirty, that swam upstream,
Branched, unfolded, spawned, evolved,
Renewed itself in a universe running down.

Outsitting three conductors, five concertmasters,
An orchestra replenishing itself
Like a body changing cells, the listener,
Clutching at last a younger elbow
To reach, just to the left, the fifteeenth row,
Besieges time that blurs from year to year,
Until the inevitable night
No player, under the stage lights' glare,
Senses the absent hearing, heartbeat and sight
That filled a particular chair.
The baton rises for the next listener there.

Departure

Such farewell gifts! no shirts
Over chairs, no waterglass on the nightstand,
The card table folded, the magazines gone,
No shaving brush glowering
Twisted from the bath: only this
Floral carpet, this bureau
Down to its wax, this bright
Bedspread awaiting
Some simpler guest. Tomorrow,
Next month, she will miss
The dry cough, the grind
Of the pencil sharpener,
The mysterious trips
To the ice tray, his john
Taming the night, but momentarily stunned
By this morning's stillness, she stops
By the open door to admire
Her extra bedroom, ringing
With clear untangled sunlight.

The Quartet Crowd

Scarce-breathing sphinxes, row on stonefaced row
Glued to the plush as if some mesmerist
Had stunned them, while onstage the four with fiddles
Bob like weeds in the wind—how can they claim
To love the sounds their bodies so resist?
Fierce listeners are one of music's riddles.
The casual, there for spouses or self-show,
Uncrinkling candies, fingering the program,
Tapping the pulse, collect their killing stare.
Their mask of elevation is a sham
To shield a wobbly edifice whose walls
Are time refashioned into space, a dream
Of motive, motion, theme and countertheme,
A form so fragile and interior
The least snapped handbag or insistent whisper
Snuffs out a stanchion and the vision falls.
They come as masons to a shrine of air.

Money: A Primer

Money, children, was invented to symbolize
Precise amounts of bread.
Instead of hauling jars of grain from here to there
We transferred clam shells instead.

Staples were set at exact sums of money.
A cow was five coins with the head of the prince.
A canoe was one crisp watermarked Isis.
No one has understood it since.

From the first, money spoke only
To other money. For instance, no Frenchman
Ever communicated with the franc
The way francs speak to marks with perfect comprehension.

But money only pretended to be jars of grain.
Money was time, scarcity, the capitalist yoke,
Security, ruin, or evidence of salvation,
Depending on who spoke.

Money is our common global language,
As current as currency,
Yet decoding efforts have proved it less tractable
Than tree rings or Linear B.

Degrees are conferred, chairs awarded, prizes delivered
In Stockholm to those who have shown
That the eerily incestuous system of money
Should be managed or left alone.

The aforementioned have yet to explain how money
Springs from its own symbolic loins.
Words have never come up with words the way
Coins coin coins.

Freed from the drudgery of mere barter, money
Has pursued an intricate course
Through consortiums, cartels, and multinationals
With the opacity of a natural force.

Money is a crude obsession with things,
Claims the anti-materialist schism.
This, at least, can be flatly declared wrong.
Money is mysticism.

Global Cleansing

The Third World is a trash fire set
By the First World. Heap huaraches and tires
And flash cubes on the teak and mahogany,
A conflagration to repay the debt.
Let the cow and canopy cross wires.
Doze the loam and humus to ignite
The leopard. Let the hummingbirds blaze out.
Train the burning glass on the parasite.
Fuse the Sphinx and the sphinx moth, manatee
And man, the last pachyderm and mahout
Into rockets to appall the crowd.
Once lianas, algae, Second World yaks,
Hibiscus, cholera and killer bee
And crania from the Great Rift, the whole tax-
onomic mess is torched with gasoline
And gone up in smoke, the plates will be allowed
To shift for themselves, having been licked clean.

Franconia Man

Holding his stone reserve
Twelve hundred feet above
The stalled interstate,
His gape is held in place
By sixteen steel pins
While a deep steel beam
Braces the five-ton brow—
Lest the blind fingers
Of wind and rain erase
What blindness brought about.
Every Fourth of July
A bridge crew supervisor
Swings from a wooden chair
To probe whether last year's ice
Has shivered the flinty eyes,
The Mohawk nose, the patrician
Chin and tight-lipped stare,
While news teams track below.
Nearing the cliff's base
Four lanes still squeeze to two,
Lest quaking transportation
Ring the Old Man down.
Locals, sightseers, friends
Fondly decelerate,
Fundraise, lobby the feds,
Petition, write letters, pray—
Whatever it takes to brace
From chance, machinery and time
That crumbling human face.

Murray

What of those who abandon their weight to chairs
Full knowing you can't simultaneously fix
A particle's motion and place: who keep their balance
Buttressed by flesh revealed to be a chance
Averaging of events that can't be assured;
Informed that possibly massless particles
Pommel the most Nobeled cerebral cortex
Finding nobody at home; those, that is,
For whom this headlong cosmos fanned and thinned
From the tiniest asymmetries way back when,
And will keep on thinning into oblivion
Until more matter shows up; who find their own
Curiosity a most curious occurrence,
Mere pattern chasing pattern, pooled ambition
Storming that reclusive elegance,
The simplest way to corner the complex?
What if you were the man who posited quarks?

He travels around the globe looking at birds.
His lifelist corners half the surviving species
While, en route, he annexes the world's
Tales to date, its politics, its jokes,
Its sauces, its diseases, its interiors,
Its braided languages and its unraveling
Habitats, for which he contrives some grants.
The world, in turn, extends its elegance
In the form of his favorite bird, the elegant trogon:
Each year, come spring, he joins an unpredictable
Mass of fellow birders at the South Fork
Of Cave Creek, where the bird preens its iridescence
On the campground john, casually scattering photons
Into the magnification of paired ground lenses
That jam its fire into the rods and cones
Of awestruck eyes, while whispering into the whorls
Of Murray's all-deciphering ears, *quark, quark* ...

Birder

Homo avephilus. Abundant. Binocular-eyed.
Plumage: camouflage, from drab green to plain
Brown. Flightless. Note characteristic guide
Book, pad, pencil. Common name: birdbrain.

Solitary to semi-gregarious. Cries include
Psssht, tsuc-tsuc, whshee whshee, tseeet,
Rrrrrrk, plus sibilant kissing of back of hand
Projecting squeaks, generic warbles: not quite

St. Francis's sermon, but draws avian audience.
Typical bonding song: do you need a yellow-rumped?
Distress call: What *was* that? Most common disease:
Linnaean Syndrome, confusion of bird-love with regard

For higher numbers, leading to competitions
Pitting sum of purported sightings against
Constraints of time and place. Attendant neck pains.
Goal: Extension of range through personal life-list,

Mythic habitat staked out in words
The subject dies compiling. Frequently-invoked
Epitaph: Of the world's 9000 birds
He logged a modest fourth before he croaked.

Enigma Variations

When the spaniel twice my age turned stiff,
My father took me aside:
Prince will be going away for awhile ...
Since our dog didn't travel alone, I
Caught my first lie.

My aunt slipped into the hospital,
Then our relatives gathered in strange clothes:
We're off to tell Ethel goodbye.
We'll say goodbye for you too, and
Someday you'll understand.

The Elgar slipped out of my hands.
Variations that nailed me to a toy chair
Sailed in black spikes
Over waxed linoleum. From then on
I knew the meaning of gone.

That lesson, in fact, I had to unlearn.
The tunes get recorded over and over
For music is pattern, not a brittle black plate.
With vinyl and tape and laser to thank,
I hear Elgar and go blank.

Spaniels, I've found, while they don't exactly repeat,
Can be replaced. As for an aunt,
Before I listened, her variation was lost.
I was the budding Stokowski, whereas
All her heroes played jazz.

Now nears that someday when I should understand.
The master tune, we probably agree,
Is memory,
All sound mere variation. I buy
New releases, a fresh try.

Opus 28, The Preludes

Key		Key
C	Beyond the keyboard's ivory portico	
	Acedia unwinters, limps its slow	a
	Pavane into a mist of gnats and mint:	G
e	Endure, it begs, spring fever's strummed lament.	
D	Spectrums of tumbled glass (*Il pleure dans mon coeur*)	b
A	In formal sadness or demonic blur	f#
	Tumble from the heart's arisen sea;	
E	Midsummer squares away its majesty:	
c#	Mazurkas of falling water; a hummingbird's	B
	Evanescence in major and minor thirds;	
g#	Volcanic stamina that overflows	
	Its stammer toward ambiguous repose;	
F#	Lagoon of cradled stars; whirlwind of dread;	eb
Db	Beauty and terror on a single thread;	
	Exhilarations racketing pell-mell	bb
	Through neural mazes of the astonished will;	
Ab	Nostalgia's tolling bronze; a summer squall's	f
	Stamped foot; soaring tracery that recalls	Eb
	The long apprenticeship of seeming ease;	
c	Steps of a season failing by degrees	
Bb	Into one last aria before	
g	The agitated aftervoices pour	
	Their chilling pulses and harmonic shocks	
F	Into Chopin's closing music box,	
d	Saving one hid fuse of energy	
	To detonate death's thrice-dissolving D.	

Embryo Transplant

Cows, stimulated by hormones and then bred,
Produce from none to sixty-seven embryos,
Each one about half the size of this period.

A catheter is inserted into the cow's
Anesthetized cervix, then an inflatable cup
Literally milks out the embryos.

The seeds can then be implanted in any group
Of diversified cows, and through one favored bull
The herd in a few short years can be shaped up.

"Seen one embryo transplant, you've seen them all,"
Says a bored transplanter. "The same," I replied, "may be said
Quite soon for your cows." As we laughed I felt my seed
Curl back, my eyes shrink from the years ahead.

Don't Ask

Illness is so boring to one's friends.
The luscious entrail readings you recite
(The cough has eased, the pain has edged to the right)
Stun your auditors, a phase that tends

To self-correct as imperceptibly
The leading question trails into the caring
Glance (translation: thank you for not sharing).
Baudelaire's diagnosis, *c'est l'ennui,*

Skewers all but a diehard few who stick
To their cheerful grilling of your ups and downs.
You humor them until the horror dawns:
Pathology engrosses them. They're sick.

Tight-lipped at last, initiate with a wealth
Of signals and stigmata now taboo,
Your secret undervoices melt into
A silence indistinguishable from health.

Death Florentine

When Dante starts again up Purgatory
This time without his shadow, with no fancy guide
To still his heart and explicate the story,

Will the spirits still crowd around him, poke his side
And exclaim, not you again! How did it go
With that opus we bared our sins for? At least you died

This time to get here. Where's your sidekick from Limbo?
Am I in a canto? I think you forgot to tell
My daughter to speed me with prayers. Is life on the Arno

Still all downhill? And leisurely suffering the full
Gravity of rocks for which his sense
Of weight has been spared, the face-in-the-cornice smell

Of greed, the nailed-up sight of the envious,
Is everything filmed with the faintest *déjà vu*?
Does posthumous acedia add new vice

To run off? Can a second-timer genuinely do
Penance without an eye half-cocked to all
The slits, the secret stairs he knows how to slip through,

Blind to the sudden break when he could crawl
Past a witless angel a notch toward his Redeemer?
Does he curse his poet's gift of total recall?

Beyond all sins of the pen, how it will seem a
Grace apart to be done with this peak he set
So exactingly down for us climbers in terza rima,

To be dragged once more through Lethe, and truly forget.

Smoke and Mirrors

Eels elaborately skilled
At vamping the ivories upside down and backwards,
Syncopating the treble, teasing
Tunes from the bass,
Electrifying the silver aquarium
Of a mirror tipped overhead—
Can such dream arms belong

To round after round of song,
To cracked voices fed
By malt and menthols jazzing the back room
Of Marina's Place,
To nights like this, so forgettably pleasing,
To this turquoise-lidded old siren belting out standards,
Keeping the tip jar filled?

Social Rubato

It was one of those summer rentals
Overstocked with temperment
Holding drinks, and the failed
Pianist was holding forth:
You need good friends and the finest
Instruction you can find,
But for god's sake never confuse
Art with life and charge
One virtuoso with both.
In the stock-taking hush that followed,
Maestro, my compliments
On intercepting my glance
Across that ill-played room
With a brow's teasingly arched
Fermata, for cueing my heart's
Re-entry with your least
Downbeat of a smile.

Across, Down

The daily paper's clotted wall of words
Fusing fact and fact, cause and effect
With yesterday's fact, no longer held intact
Unless it was tucked in half and creased in thirds,
Crossword on top. Braced on a crossed knee,
Stocks, cartoons, obits mere depth to write on,
It's chronic hints—stock pun, transparent clue,
Blackbird and sloth and fescue and ossuary
No longer necessary to look up,
Skewed definition easily seen through—
Still held for words whose touch with life was gone,
Still peopled the empty squares, still played their tricks
Of intersection, weaving on his lap
A quilt of language purified of sense,
Irreducible as music or mathematics.
Head bent, mind still, bifocals glittering,
Surveying his princely grid of filled-in blanks,
My father took his verbal stand against
The nameless separation of everything.

Unfinished Roses
(NLB 1908-1989)

Five blossoms, a clear vase, a little water.
On a near table
A metal box folded open, its enamel
Tray lifted out. A water jar. Four camel
Hair brushes pinched into commas and points.
Squirming lead tubes
Cinched with bits of the spectrum. Stiff paper
On which a pencil had ghosted
Five blossoms, a clear vase, a little water.
A clipboard propped like an altar.

Moistened and touched to cadmium,
A brush's splayed hook
Bled into a petal. Squeezed dry
And rebaptized, it quickened the loop:
Jar, pigment, petal ... Soon the entire
Slab of enamel
Eddied with lake, ran with rose madder.
The water jar turned to dung.
The paper's tinder
Was touched by water into roses of fire.

Splayed hook exchanged for pliant dart.
Choked down, it dropped a line
Of lemon from a bloom. Nipped clean,
It repeated the line in blue:
A stalk in green!
Barbed and blended, each stem
Dove to the vase's drawn water.
Now bloomed the enigma at heart:
Turning roses from round to flat
Made them more perfect yet.
Mom cleaned her brushes and quit.

Petals fell in the night. Next morning
I found their likeness curled in the trash.
Hey! Aren't you going to finish ...
No, it's started wrong
And the hard part's below the water line.
But I'd caught the trick:
Pruning depth made the blossoms last.
I reclipped the paper: son would be priest!

Why introduce yellow into blue?
Unmixed hooker's green would do.
I unscrewed the cap and squeezed a gob
Into one of the tray's little stalls. The nib
Of a stem-sized brush, stabbed in the jar
And dredged in the tray, took up where
Yesterday had dried, and brought
The paint to where the pencil gave out.
Untamed innocence of the laws
Of perspective swelled the distortions of vase
And water, leaving the stem of each rose
Encased in a length of hose.
I held the result in a mat.
I, too, quit.

Metal box snapped shut, metal tubes
Drying inside, priest long defrocked,
Watercolorist gone.
On the wall, some vital signs
(Snowscape, wave, cactus, barn)
Of roses started right, but the trick
Of subtracting depth falls flat
In a medium too quick
For the realized human figure, further dashing
The likelihood of finishing anyone's lines.

sing the Gift

What could our circle have
In common to provoke
Mutual warmth in the face
Of such deep differences?
It struck me like a joke:
All of us like to laugh.

I even have to wonder
Whether I'm quite intact
Not to be quaking for sex,
Travel, praise or fat checks;
Alas, it's the naked act
Of laughter I prefer.

But more and more we lack
For anything very funny
To say of a world that's less
And less hilarious.
We settle for irony.
Wit goes sour and black.

Friends keep bantering
Along in their bravest tone,
If only around me.
I laugh compulsively,
And too often I laugh alone.
Humor's a bitter thing.

The Bates Method

It was revenge on Wednesdays to cut classes,
Board the El downtown to an unmarked vestibule
Between movie marquees, drag eleventh grade feet
Up a shadowy stairwell, down a twenty-watt hall,
Through a frosted glass door and into a pale suite
         That promised Sight Without Glasses.

Amid charts and machines and fluorescence not even I
Found it excessive that an assistant named Iris
Taught us to line up colored dots in 3-D,
To sun and palm away our conjunctivitis,
To look from a held-up pencil to the far E
         And back to firm up the eye.

Cheese sandwiches dank in the bag, it even seemed cool
To sway, lids shut, then flash on some fixed bum
Down on Randolph Street—and if eye before E was a bore,
If some reported Dramatic Improvements while some
Merely disappeared, even shifting myopics were more
         Enlightening than school.

The doctor gave thanks I was coming along so fast,
Conjunctivitis all cleared, and didn't I test
Better on the chart? Well, a bit, perhaps. But where
Was the assistant? On her way to a long-needed rest ...
A disappearance the doctor was soon to share:
         Next week would be her last.

As the sibyl under the sunlamp hissed, how could
That wretch she kept by her side ten years, so kind
And drab, so dedicated, all sweetness and scruple,
That Iris have, well, stolen the doctor blind?
Wednesday's child was once more the dim pupil,
         Near-sighted for good.

Explaining Ellie

Trimming the shrubs, I thought how my late aunt
Found all things surgical so glamorous.
Driving ambulance for the Red Cross
Ripened dashingly into incessant
Fundraising, board meetings, a new wing
For therapy, a coveted heart surgeon,
Collages for the lobby, a CAT-scan—
Or else (stubbing a Kool) it was this string
Of accidents and ills befalling all
Mutual friends, not sparing horses, dogs,
Herself: glaucoma, skin grafts, bone spurs, legs
Yowling ever since that teenage fall
Steeplechasing: our tomboy in the sun,
Our redhead who metasticized out loud
In monologues that drove the family mad.
A clap of shears: there was my aunt newborn.
Helpless, would-be bundle of concern,
Her older sister, five, still held the show,
Struck one year before with polio.
Illness was the wordless trick to learn,
Was care, was being irresistably sick.
Upstart, beauty, scholar, champion
Of ice and saddle, she outlived the one
Who took her childhood, but foreclosure struck
So deeply that they probably could put
Her name in Guinness for the summer she
Pushed back the frontiers of pathology
And snared malaria in Connecticut.
Enough to freeze a nephew, reaching out
With rusty blades, hoping her hospital
Would patch me back together if I fell
From shaky steps, unbalanced by the thought
Of how a past comes passionately clear
With one lost piece in place, so obvious,

So clarifying, and perhaps so false.
This summing of the speechless: was it fair?
Leaning recklessly for one last limb,
I wondered how my living kin would like
Their cousin's contribution to pop psych.
Never had the lilacs been so trim.

The Wedding Gift

A foot coiled back, an arm outstretched,
And in her backward hand the thin
Impossibly long, exquisitely tapered javelin
That waits like ivory lightning over
The little marble pedestal to be launched
Into the lucky future—

It gleams through childish eyes against
Its athletic shadow, the lone *objet*
Enshrined on the mantel, and I still hear my mother say
On the stations of the house tour, *This*
Is our Diana, our household spirit, a present
From Eleanor and Chris.

It must have been after my own departure
Yet well before my father's death
That a cleaning lady snapped the javelin's upper half
And junked the evidence in panic,
Leaving an irrationally crouching figure
Trailing an ugly spike,

And it might have been the house-breaking just
After my mother's remarriage, or yet
Some further dislocation even I forget
When the reliable Brisk & Brusque
Moving Co. knocked off the rest
Of that endangered tusk.

Now gripping what no stranger could guess
Is a thonged handle, her limbs can be seen
Among clocks and coasters, an ivory dancer in a green
Tunic, demoted to the shade
Of one more house, Olympian and useless,
Poised with her grenade.

Back East

A sip of Ballantine's Ale is the madeleine
To take me back to the shores of Twin Lakes again.
It sprawled from the rotting underside of the pier,
Ragweed and mint, the willow overgrown,
A childhood running out as the place ran down—
It curries my nostrils again, fervent and clear.
A sip of Ballantine's Ale is the madeleine
But it was being ruined by outboards even then.

You could tour that whole place by the sense of smell—
The tea cart full of old sweaters, machine oil, the well
Cranking out iron, rancid shower stalls
And cedar closets, the complicated stench
Of dahlias by the fly-specked screens on the porch,
Woodsmoke, dawn's sweet stab of cinnamon rolls,
The boathouse of mildewed cement with its reeking store
Of gasoline, fish knives, peroxide, weeds by the shore—

My brother went back to see it. The folks were quite nice
And showed him how they'd doubled the asking price
By subdividing the badminton and croquet;
Meanwhile they'd cleared out the hickories to let in the sun,
And hauled out that tangle of weeds so the lawn could run
Right down to the lake, where their sixty-five horsepower lay
In state by the stainless sweep of their metal pier.
I dream of the days Back East, nursing my beer.

⌣f Joe

When Jerry died, the inhabiting spirit went out
Of Joe. Candles no longer flickered about
The blues singers he'd known, nor did he care
That years ago he'd danced for Agnes de Mille.
Expelled from the past, wholly unaware
Of present affliction, he hauled himself weekdays to
His bookkeeping job at the prison, and in his cups
He no longer sang *Deep In The Dream Of You.*
It's stunned us all, this dissolution that stops
Short of the flesh, for on Sundays we can still
Batter our love against his barside trance
Of scotch and silence, an abiding wreath
Of smoke around this stone continuance
Of Joe, our single proof of life after death.

Window Seats

I am tired of staring down on my country from planes,
Tired of inwardly stitching the cockeyed quilt
Of the East, the spacious Mondrians of the Great Plains,
The crumpled-up West—I turn at last without guilt

To my book and my three-dollar wine. Not that it's dull
To learn those astral circles in Kansas were made
By wheeling sprinklers, to watch full reservoirs trail
Dried riverbeds like old string, to note how road chases road

In replications more parallel than hacks
In a cutting board. I've found unlooked-for peace
As our long Midwestern shadow overtakes
The theatrics of basin and range, and deeper hypnosis

As town after nameless town disappear through the dark
Like unraveling crossword puzzles. But the shapes all distill
To a headful of theorems. I turn to my wine and my book
And keep my travel camouflaged until

The personalized farewells of flight attendants
Exhale me to freedom, out of our jammed-up slot,
To walk the accordian tubing into a concourse
Where sometimes someone is waiting. Usually not.

Practice Rooms

Along a basement hall
Where loners pommel and knead
Cheap spinets, the drilled phrase
Strains to perfection.
Cell by cell,
Leap by cadenza by run
Between walls like sonic mirrors,
Music in solitary confinement
Breaks through plaster, redoubles, interferes
Into the warring tribute dissonance
Accords to harmony,
And a balked player stops
Cold. This is the moment
Of aural bleed,
Of letting all frequencies
Pour through the wall
And roar through blanked-out nerve and mind and skin.
Such hands home to the keys,
Letting the jammed strain
Fly from the fingertips
Unerring, free,
More fervent than it ever will again.

Late Sibelius

When a tree fell in Finland, Sibelius scored
The after-silence. There a strain began
That sang between the hammer-blows of brass,
That gaped beyond the last chromatic winds,
Promising cold comfort in the full
Cadence of a returning Age of Ice
When silence begins *attacca*.
                              Biographers
Variously account for the thirty years
Between the composer's death and the death of the man:
State subsidy. Drink. Throat cancer from cigars.
Innovation insufficiently avant-garde.
Neglect, exhaustion, compositional impasse,
Geographic backwash, all the compacted
Disconnections brought to a final ripeness
In the full silence of the awaited Eighth
Promised, denied, destroyed. Or never begun,
And whose familiar themes compose us still
In blizzarding TVs and jammed circuits,
In sirens, distant playgrounds, sonic booms,
In your very refrigerator cranking out ice
Or, if you're luckier, in waves on the shore
And wind through the pines, all your encompassing folklore
Dismantled, cross-examined, pulled apart
And packed again from its constituent parts.
This is his symphony that most endures.
Put this down and listen to late Sibelius.

Pomp and Consequence

When you graduate fearful and teary-eyed from whatever
Institution has wound your literary
Spring, worried less about getting a job
Than breaking the spell, letting go of kids
Now closer than kin, planning to get together
In that dim adulthood where friendship never ends,

Make sure, if you plan to pull it off, that you end
Up like they do. Get married, hold a job,
Invest in a house, make payments, commute, have kids.
Teach and get tenure if you're at all literary,
Find a department chairman to hate, whatever—
Else you'll wind up at the next get-together

With only laughter in brackets to feign together.
When you swoop into town to kindle some literary
Binge, to exhume old wickedness, whatever
Self you flew back to confirm, they'll be taking the kids
To Little League, grading papers, contriving to end
The evening with one quick beer because of the job.

You begin to feel like a kind of reverse Job
With no blighted cattle, no ruined mansion, no kids
Whose outgrown clothing, colds, bad grades and end-
less running vendettas are less than literary.
Despairing of common plagues to hold you together
You watch your fates unravel toward whatever

Separates old inseparables forever.
Now terrified less all communion end
In Christmas cards, never to get together
Year upon year no matter how bad a job
You make of it, you appropriate the kids'
Playroom lethal with four-wheeled litter, airy

With brow-thumping mobiles, watching your literary
Sleep-ins endured while your generous host is ever
Trying to keep up with wife, new friends and job
On the hangovers you still incur together.
Is he too unwilling to let the past deadend?
Or are you the only one the present kids?

At cocktails together you're still a couple of kids,
But he has a job to think of while you are forever
The endless houseguest upon the earth, literary.

Staying Up

Still on top
Sharp as a tack,
Mind like a trap,
Never misses a trick—

So we speak
Of the clear-eyed elder
Whose flesh has shrunk
To a grip on a walker,

Pared to an ever-
Contracting show
And hyperaware
Of you right now.

The octo-, the nona-
genarian
Appears to grow
By holding on

As we decline,
Sustained success
An unbroken
Consciousness.

They overtake us,
Standing out
By getting no worse,
Their single point

To hold one point
Resilient and sharp,
Their quiet stunt
Staying up

Nights without sleep,
Their final prank
Just to keep
Their keepers awake.

Vespers

How civilized to get sloshed mid-afternoon
       And blunder into St. John the Divine
Where nurseries of neck-breaking columns steel the brain,
       Where Christ's red robes at the end of the apse
Glisten like stained glass chiles: where it feels fine
       To pick a pew and collapse!

Nuns are blurring some winged and sheeted first-graders
       Across my field of vision, crisply
Telling them to 'develop their characters'—
       Mercifully just pageant practise,
Not survival training, nor can the cherubim see
       This tourist in from the cactus

Free-associating from farewell rites
       With a long-missed Eastern friend. Chance,
Sings a nun in *Dialogues of the Carmelites*,
       Is the logic of God—phrase that recurs
From last night's opera here where the cool brilliance
       Of His non sequiturs

Bends into chords of light the dizzying skies
       Of this island where a subway stair
Now leads you to a locked gate and hostile eyes,
       Where home to the new refugee is five
Shopping bags, where locals for whom I care
       Perilously survive

By rites of anti-communion as day declines.
       Windows, drained of their stories,
Might be veins of ruby and sapphire in a mine,
       Anywhere deep enough to deaden
That thousand-tongued, most tabloid of allegories,
       The countdown to Armageddon.

Decompression ends with a small bell—
        A staccato whisper above me—
Puerto Rican, perhaps a real Gabriel
        As if the naturalized rose window
Itself regretted this public sanctuary
        Closed until tomorrow.

Myoptics

The cicadas of summer sing all year
        In my left ear.
I muscle toward the future clad
        In a heating pad.

Sight becomes astigmatism
        Through a double prism.
The springs of insolence are found
        By ultrasound.

Solid rock dissolves through strata
        Of dissolving data.
I'll tell you what the near-sighted see:
        Entropy.

But Time

Was it the poster of the isle,
The round trip ticket's special rate,
Luggage that I packed in style,
Cacciatore that I ate
With Merlot on a plastic plate?
Choices passed in pantomime
Like turnoffs on the interstate.
What flew me to Kauai but time?

Unthinking childhood's one-time trial
Of chicken pox may incubate
Along the brain stem all this while,
Nerving itself to detonate,
Four unthinking decades late,
New aches, new rashes; and though I'm
On pills, I still interrogate,
What makes us wrong or right but time?

Unthinking fingers spin the dial.
Discrimination takes the bait
Of strings and oboes. Yes, you smile,
The shrieks, the silence meant to state
A randomness so out-of-date—
Replay it and the same will chime.
A theme heard once is also Fate.
Decomposition too is time.

Gravity could loom so great
It stops expansion on a dime,
Reversing time, they speculate.
But what will bring us back but time?

These Arias

The last shower you take in a favorite house,
A novel whose pleasures you'll never repeat, one flawless
Sunset watch the evening before departure—
This inflammation of the unceasing lastness
Of every untorn thing will rend your heart,
Will hollow icy halls for melancholy
To draw its deadly whisper through your marrow
Repeating useless, useless the way *addio*
Runs through Itialian opera, its plaintive cadence
Crumbling into the wings, vanquished by Clio.
These arias can only be ridden out.
Farewell irreplaceable shirt. Goodbye old car.
Forgive tomorrow's absence, fond cafe.
Poor faithful chair, abandoned at Goodwill.
And you, unexpected friend. *Addio. Addio.*